Keep Calm and Ask On

A No-Nonsense Guide to
Fulfilling Your Dreams

By
Michael Samuels

Disclaimer

The information in this book is not to be used to treat or diagnose any particular disease or any particular patient. The author is not engaged in rendering professional advice or services to the individual reader. The ideas, procedures, and suggestions contained in this book are not intended as a substitute for consulting a health care advisor. All matters regarding your health require medical supervision. If you decide to take part in any of the activities listed in this book, you do so at your own risk. Several of the activities listed here can be very dangerous, and you should seek out a qualified instructor before trying them. The author is not liable or responsible for any loss or damage allegedly arising from any information or suggestions in this book.

Grateful Acknowledgments

To Kevin and Stu, the funniest guys in the Universe

To Hallie and Zachary: the Universe could not have given me a more loyal and loving niece and nephew

Special Shout-Out

To Matthew and Steven: thank you both for keeping me young at heart

Follow Michael

@UniverseMichael

www.samuelsbooks.com

If you find this book enjoyable, I really hope that you'll leave a review on Amazon, Goodreads or Barnes & Noble under *Keep Calm and Ask On*. If you have any questions or comments, please contact me directly at Michael@samuelsbooks.com.

Other books by Michael:

Just Ask the Universe – A No-Nonsense Guide to Manifesting Your Dreams

The Universe-ity – A Spiritual Education Using the Law of Attraction

Table of Contents

Intro

"Never be in a hurry; do everything quietly and in a calm spirit. Do not lose your inner peace for anything whatsoever, even if your whole world seems upset."
—Saint Francis de Sales

"When adversity strikes, that's when you have to be the most calm. Take a step back, stay strong, stay grounded, and press on."
—LL Cool J

"Calm can solve all issues."
—Pope Shenouda III

Hey there! It's me; I'm back. And I'm so pleased that you decided to pick up my new book *Keep Calm and Ask On*. I cannot begin to tell you the amount of joy I've received over the past few years since the release of *Just Ask the Universe* and *The Universe-ity*. People from all over the world have written me and thanked me for showing them the way: getting the job they wanted, getting the soul mate that was waiting for them, or getting the cash flow that would allow them to live a life of freedom. I know that all of these desires sound vague. But they exist, and universally, everyone has the same wants.

I am so blessed to be able to bring you my newest edition, titled *Keep Calm and Ask On*. Please know that this is not a sequel to my other books. This book will stand alone, but I will refer to many points that I made in *Just Ask the Universe*. So, if you're new here, don't worry; I will explain everything. And if you've read my previous work, don't worry because I won't ramble on.

In researching and dealing with people, I've learned something very crucial: people want simplicity. They want to get from point *A* to point *B* in the easiest and most convenient way possible. There is nothing wrong with this. What can be said effectively in one hundred pages sounds much better than just dragging on and on and on in two hundred pages.

Simply put, I'm not a scientist. I'm a person who works in his family business and creates everything I want with my subconscious mind. I'm not a billionaire; I don't live in a twenty-thousand-square-foot mansion on the Gold Coast of Long Island. I honestly don't even own a watch. I drive a four-year-old SUV that I absolutely adore and have fun in my life on a day-to-day basis. I have a beautiful wife, two wonderful children, loving parents, and a loyal brother, sister-in-law, niece, and nephew. My life is pretty great.

People from all over want to know if they can become billionaires...or be famous...or drive really expensive cars. If these are some of your wants, then good for you. *But why do you really want them?* We are going to explore this.

My favorite letters are from people who sabotage. They buy a good "law of attraction" book, try to do the exercises in the book, wait a day, and then write to me and tell me how nothing works. Well, this new book is for all of you out there who desire answers.

People just simply cannot keep calm. They are not getting enough rest. They are focused too much on what they don't have and should be focused on what they do have. There was a reason why I wanted you to write an "I Gratefully Received It" list in *Just Ask the Universe*. There are things in this world that you have received, and you have asked for them in the correct manner. People need to relax and take a deep breath to make sure that they know what they want, why they want it, and how they are going to attain it. It's simple enough to write down your wants. You really have to understand why you want them. Just saying that you want to be a billionaire means absolutely nothing to the Universe.

My other favorite letter I receive is from people who write that they are confused if they write "I want" or "I am" or "I have." We will clear all of that up once and for all too.

Nothing should be confusing about the law of attraction. You should be laughing about it. Speaking of laughing, we're going to touch upon how laughter really *is* the key in any law of attraction technique.

This is another practical guide to fulfilling your dreams. I will try to spare as much fluff and mysticism as I can. So let's get those gears moving and just remember: keep calm and ask on.

Chapter 1

There Will Be Wants

"Where sense is wanting, everything is wanting."
—Benjamin Franklin

"Happiness isn't getting what you want; it's wanting what you got."
—Garth Brooks

"Everybody talks about wanting to change things and help and fix, but ultimately all you can do is fix yourself. And that's a lot. Because if you can fix yourself, it has a ripple effect."
—Rob Reiner

Everyone has wants, needs, goals, objectives, wishes, requests, requirements, demands, and desires. These words are pretty interchangeable. When I say everyone, I mean that *everyone* on this planet has wants. Your wants probably differ from other people's wants, but they're there. You can't escape them. You want something right now—right this instant. You could be hungry; you could be thirsty. You could be tired. You may want to clean your closet. Okay, probably not. You could want a million dollars. That sounds more like it!

Everyone, since the history of our amazing Universe began, has wanted something. Our ancestors wanted basic things in life, like food and shelter. We wouldn't be here if it weren't for them.

We wouldn't be here today if it weren't for our mothers and fathers and their mothers and fathers and their...well, you get the picture. Let's expand our minds a bit and keep thinking back to the dawn of humankind. They wanted something, which led to a new generation of people that wanted something, which continued down the line of human evolution and history, until it got here to you today. Wherever you are reading this book—the bedroom, the kitchen, the train—you are here, right now, living your life because your ancestors *wanted* something.

What's wrong with wanting things? Absolutely nothing. We are a species of wants. It boggles my mind from the letters that I receive from people saying, "Shouldn't we say we have it?" "Aren't we confusing our subconscious minds by saying, 'I want?'"

Well, shouldn't our ancestors have spoken aloud that they already had food, when there was nothing to eat? No. They sharpened their spears and hunted for food. They wanted something, and in the act of survival, *they took action!*

You aren't here today—physically here today—if your ancestors didn't take action. They wanted to survive. They didn't say to themselves, "I am surviving," while being chased by a saber-toothed tiger. They ran like crazy to make sure that you would be here.

Let's fast forward a few million years—say, to like fifty years ago. What about your folks? You wouldn't be here today if you didn't have a mother and father. Your mom and dad could be the most selfish people in the world; you may have never even known your mother and father, but you're still here. They took action and created you. They made you! And their parents made them. And your great-grandparents made them—again, you get the picture.

What am I trying to say here?

Everyone *wants* something. Let's take something as simple as a steak. I love steak. For me to think that I am eating a steak right now will just make me hungrier. To picture the steak sitting right in front of me, smelling all nice and juicy and amazing, will do absolutely nothing for me. So what would be the most logical thing to do? It would be for me to get up, go to the freezer, take out a steak, defrost it, grill it, and eat it.

I could say that the Universe gave me that steak. I wanted something. I thought it. I got off my behind and cooked it. Luckily, my wife and kids weren't home; otherwise, I'd have to have shared it. Just kidding—I love sharing with my family, especially the vegetables.

Okay, so back to my "want" thesis. We all want something, and there is nothing wrong with that. Our ancestors wanted to survive, so they ate meat and built shelter. Could you imagine a Neanderthal thinking in his head, "I am living in a beautiful thatched hut made of off-white wooly mammoth tusks and café au lait deer skin." But in the meantime, it's the Ice Age; his family is freezing their butts off, and he's thinking he already has it? In certain colors, I may add.

Can't this be likened to your situation today? We may only be a blip in between Ice Ages, but what is your financial situation like? Are you thinking, "I am a billionaire, and I'm the envy of all my friends, and I buy whatever I want?" You know that this isn't the correct way of doing something. You'd be thinking like our ancestors who didn't survive—who didn't take action. They were freezing their butts off, waiting for something to happen.

The first great discovery humans made was when they could think. This was the day when they first said, "I want." This marked their first day of personal attainment. From that day, humans evolved further than any invention imaginable and had to make all further progress themselves. From that day, there was no necessary evolution; they had to work in conscious alignment with life. As the result of the discovery that they could think, plan, and implement, people have built up a great civilization; we have realized that the Universe works through us in order to serve us. We have harnessed electricity, compelled steam to do our bidding, conquered the air, built cities, made the desert to bloom, and thrown the lines of commerce around the globe.

Humans' first discovery of their ability to think was taken as a matter of fact. We have always been able to think. It was proof that it existed; it gave us the ability to know our needs and supply them. It appeared to be an automatic thing: it came with us wherever we went. It has always been there, ready to serve our needs. We just had to learn to use it correctly.

You cannot think the words *I have* or *I own* and not have or own anything. It makes no sense. And you're going to confuse the hell out of your subconscious mind.

I have a million dollars. But you're living in a rented basement. Saying that I have it will make you discouraged, because you really don't have it. And the way that you're asking for it, you probably won't ever have it.

How could you say that you have something and it's really not there? You are not setting a goal for yourself, and that is really all that a "want" is. Your "wants" are your goals, and they have to be set carefully and correctly for them to come true. So I'm putting to bed here this thought: don't say, "I have." Because you really don't have it. What you have is a goal of attaining it. That is what your subconscious wants to hear. Your subconscious doesn't have things; it creates things. It wants to give you the things that you want. It wants to create things just for you. If you think that you have it and it doesn't come to fruition, you will get discouraged and so will your subconscious mind.

We cannot live in a choiceless life. Every day, every moment, every second, there is choice. If it were not so, we would not be human.

We have the right to choose what we wish to feel and to experience. We have the right to choose the kind of companions we wish to connect with, to live in what city and in what type of house we would like to live.

There can be no choice unless there is something from which to choose; otherwise, the ability to choose would be merely a fantasy. A particular and precise intelligent idea in your mind will produce a particular and precise actual manifestation identical to itself. There is one Universe but a limitless numbers of forms, which change as the specific idea in the mind behind them changes.

Thoughts are things, and they have the power to objectify themselves.

In reality, there is no limitation. Your mind has the power to make a tree out of an acorn. You just have to plant it and water it. The Universe knows no difference between a million dollars and a penny. It only does what it is told.

What you have to do is set your wishes, your goals, your wants correctly. You have to know that although you don't have that particular thing now, your subconscious and the Universe will work hand in hand to materialize it for you.

It's not all about fancy boats and Rolex watches. What's important is growth and spirituality. Well, that's broad, you may say. It's really not. Growth is constant and never-ending improvement in life. If you don't think, you don't grow. If you don't take action, you don't grow. If you don't expand your mind, you won't get to the next level. And when you get to the next level, it's not over. There is another level after that.

I knew a guy who said, "Someday, if I can just make a salary of $100,000 a year, I will be the happiest guy in the world." Guess what? He followed my advice, set his wants, commanded his subconscious, and got the salary. Lo and behold, the guy was still miserable. Now he wanted more.

Growth is natural, just like wants. If you think for one instant that I wrote a worldwide best-selling book and now I'm done with growing, you are 100 percent wrong. I wanted to learn more and expand my mind into other arenas of spirituality.

Now, back to this guy. After he made a hundred-thousand-dollar salary, he didn't think it was enough. So he asked for more from the Universe, and the Universe delivered. And guess what? He still wasn't happy. I asked my friend, "Why are you even asking for things if it isn't making you happy?" And you know what he said to me? He said, "Michael, every time I get my goal, I think that will make me happy, and it doesn't." So I said, "What if you actually enjoyed the moment, the journey, and you took every day to get to that $100,000? And once you hit that want, how about betting bigger and enjoying a new portion of your journey?" A light bulb went off for him. It wasn't getting the money that made him happy. It was who he became during the journey that mattered the most!

Who are you becoming on your journey to your wants? What are some of your wants that you want to accomplish that will bring joy and satisfaction in your life? Perhaps you want to open a business and offer employment to hundreds of people and get the feeling that you are helping put food on thousands of people's tables. You can't say, "I want to run a big business and be rich and famous."

Why?

Why do you want these things? What will you feel when you get there? What do you want to be like when you arrive at your destination in a brand new Mercedes? Having a Mercedes must be amazing, but why do you want it? For status? For a symbol of being rich? To show off?

"Why" is the key question that I left out in *Just Ask the Universe*. We are digging deeper here, and I want you to stay with me on this. Getting "stuff" from the Universe is easy. It's not hard whatsoever, but why do you want it?

Why are "wants" in our lives so significant? With wants, we create our purpose. We invent our future in advance. We get the desired outcome. We get the object. We shape our lives. We get to tell the story of our lives. And there is someone who really wants to hear about our story. It's the Universe! The Universe wants to sit and listen to everything about your life and your story. But, we're going to be really careful how we tell the story to the Universe. We don't want the Universe to get frightened or confused. We want a clear, concise, and fun story. The Universe is sitting right now in your living room, den, car, or wherever you're reading or listening to this book. It wants to hear all about you. First, we have to talk about those wants.

We all have wants, whether we know it or not. The problem is that some people have really lousy wants. And whatever your wants are, they are affecting you. Maybe your wants are just to get by. Maybe your wants are just to finish the week. Maybe your wants are to pay the monthly bills. The problem with wants like that is that they don't actually stir you and get you to jump out of bed early in the morning to say, "I can't wait to go out today and pay my bills."

Does paying bills create energy in people? We already know the answer to that. Desires can give us the ability to produce our achievements. But we must have something out there that's convincing enough to attract us forward. We need to have an object in our story that makes us want to get there.

Decide what prop in your story is important to you and take huge steps every day, even though it doesn't seem like it's working. Success doesn't happen without failures. Wants should give you something to look forward to every day.

I can tell you that in my own life, wants have changed me. You can learn all the methods of attaining things, but if you don't know why you're doing it, if you don't know what you're moving toward, then it's rare that you're going to get the most out of yourself.

Years ago I began to study how to manifest your dreams. I was chasing unwanted relationships. I was unhealthy; I didn't have my life where I wanted it in terms of my business, but when I awoke and started listening to people who were smarter than I was, I began to set my wants in my journal. Then all I did was ask the Universe to deliver them. Believe me when I tell you: I set wants that were *impossible*.

I had no idea how I was going to make them happen. But I worked from a ground rule. You must have confidence in *trust*: trust in the Universe; trust in love; trust in your friends; trust in your family; trust in yourself; trust in attaining everything you want. If you don't trust, your efforts will be useless.

If you discover a want that stirs your soul, then the Universe will figure out how to make it happen. Even though it may not seem feasible, you must have trust that the Universe will pull it off.

When you lay out wants for your life in every subject—mentally, spiritually, and physically—the Universe will deliver. This is what the Universe wants for you. It wants to give you things. It wants to help you create the life that you desire. But how are you reacting when asking for these things? Are you controlling your emotions, or are you acting out of control? Are you conducting yourself from a place of faith, loyalty, and trust? Or are you miserable, deceitful, and dishonest?

Recognize the following: if you can get in control of your reactions, you can get everything you want.

Set wants on how you want to be: how you want to connect with people; how much enjoyment you want to experience; how much desire you long for. How do you want to live every single day in your life?

When you write out your wants, the Universe will know what to work with, but you *must* change. Colossal transformation must be made in your life, and the Universe will go well beyond the call to create everything you've ever dreamed of.

I received an e-mail recently from a woman, asking me, "Why is it that some

people who are honest and good suffer
so much, and the evil people prosper?"
I don't know exactly what she meant
by "good"; perhaps she meant it from a
shallow standpoint that these people were
spiritual, honest in business dealings, kind
to neighbors, gave to charity, were good
to their families, and practiced the rituals
and rites of their religious beliefs. Maybe
she meant by "evil people" those who are
unspiritual, who have no religious affiliations,
who cheat and steal, who drink and do
drugs. If so, her thinking was very superficial.

The alleged "evil" people may believe in
success, prosperity, and good health, and
they get whatever they believe. The Universe
doesn't hold one person in reverence while
disrespecting the other. The sun shines on
the just and the unjust. The Universe has no
standards. A rude person can swim in water;
that same water will support and sustain him
or her as well as a nice person. A cutthroat
business tycoon can breathe the air just as
well as the spiritually enlightened person.
The supposed honest and good person

may secretly harbor obnoxious and spiteful thoughts, and he or she will bring all the suffering upon himself or herself with his or her destructive thinking.

It is not what a person does externally for show that matters. It is the inner undertaking of the heart that counts. It is what that individual thinks, feels, and believes deep down in his or her heart that matters—not what that person admits or owns up to believing. A person may perceive all the principles, rules, and regulations of his or her place of worship; he or she may attend every ceremony and ritual, give candy to children, and donate money to the charities—all of which may be considered "good" from an external standpoint, but not from the standpoint of the Universe and its laws, which include, "As a person thinks in his or her heart, so he or she is." The Universe is unprejudiced and cannot give good for evil or evil for good. All evil ultimately destroys itself.

Your subconscious mind is like a recording, which reproduces whatever you have impressed upon it. This is why you are told not to fret about evildoers; their own subconscious mind reacts negatively or positively according to the use they are making of it. The point is this: use your own mind constructively and harmoniously, and don't bother about the other people—just wish them well.

Dream big dreams, acquire good morals, and realize and know that you get what you ask for. Value your wants of what you want to be and cease whining, complaining, and groaning about bad luck and good luck. Nourish that ideal of yours and imagine the Universe and its beauty draping over your wants.

The oak sleeps in the acorn; the giant sequoia tree sleeps in its tiny seed; the bird waits in the egg; and the Universe waits to give you everything you want. You will always gravitate to that which you secretly most love. You will meet in life the exact reproduction of your own thoughts. There is no chance, coincidence, or accident in a world ruled by the Universe. You will rise as high as your foremost aims, and you will descend to the level of your lowest concept of yourself.

When I learned these principles, my life transformed at every level. I had a level of confidence that I didn't think was possible. You will not imagine the types of miracles that the Universe will deliver into your life. I know this sounds like magic, but it really works.

Even if you can't control what's going on outside in the Universe, you sure as hell can control what's going on inside. You are in charge of your own subconscious mind—not the other way around. Your subconscious is the vessel that communicates with the Universe.

I remember visiting a certain beachfront city—it's my favorite place in the world, and I've been to most major cities around the globe, but this one place is the most fun and exciting city I've ever been to. I wanted to own a second home there as a vacation spot, a place to relax and to hang with friends, a place where my family would cherish amazing memories.

I never would have thought in a million years that just two years after writing this want down, I'd own a second home in a brand new development just a few feet from the beach. I go there five times a year with my wife, kids, mom and dad, my brother and his family, and a few of our best friends, and we have a ball!

And guess what I do when I'm there? I set more wants. I analyze my life and balance it and have fun. If you would have told me that two years earlier, I would have said that you were totally nuts; it's so impractical; there's just no way. Get real—a second home? On a beach?

Oh, it happened.

But, if I had told the Universe a story about my past regrets and bad experiences, I wouldn't have gone anywhere. If I had told the Universe a story about my life that sucked, that home would have been just another dream I'd be chasing.

Now, let's focus on you. The first thing you must do is to get your wants that will energize you. Wants must excite you. The first step is to write them down.

Whether it is something expressive inside of you that you want to invent, a personality revolution, an action or routine that you want to break free from, or a business that you want to start, or an amount of money you want to earn—how about a second home by the beach? I'm telling you, from personal experience, it can happen. The magic of the Universe that you've heard about and dreamed about is real.

It starts with a basic approach of taking these simplified urges of your wants and beginning to describe them with more detail. You are effectively communicating with your subconscious and, in turn, with the power of the Universe.

There is something beyond just what you write down. Something happens. A spark is lit. You become a creator when you write down your wants. That's what your subconscious and the Universe want from you. They want to help create the reality of your dreams.

We must make sure you not only set your wants but that you are definitely sure about why you want them. Why do you want more money? Why do you want more time? Why do you want all the toys in the world? There is a reason why, and we will get to that shortly.

There is a ground rule to writing down wants, and it changed my life. When I learned the following, it brought everything I wanted even closer to me.

Your drive to getting what you want is stronger than actually getting it.

The need for wants is not so that you get more vacations, more money in the bank, or the spouse of your dreams. The reason of any want—the real aim to setting your wants on paper—is what they will make of you as a person. Who will you become when you get that beach house? Who will you become when you make $100,000 a year or $100,000,000 per year?

At the end of this lifetime, all the "stuff" you accrue is not going to make you happy. At the end of your life, all you're going to have is who you've become as an individual, and that is what matters the most. What are you leaving behind for the next generation to build upon? Did you set up your family? Did you accomplish everything you wanted during your journey? And did it make you happy?

But if all you do is concentrate on getting things, the Universe won't bring anything closer to you. In their quest to get things, some people have given up the honor of who they want to be, of what they want to produce in their life. When you set a want, you must know why you are doing it.

For example, you want to make a million dollars. There is nothing wrong with this. However, just saying "I want a million dollars" can only stimulate you so much. What would you feel if you had the million dollars? What type of person would you be? What would change in your life? Having the independence you think the money will give you, having the capacity to provide, or having the capacity to do amazing things that you think that money will supply you will inspire you much more than just the money.

One issue with setting wants is that most people don't take it seriously, and they don't do it constantly.

They get enthusiastic about the want itself, and for a while, they are pretty excited. And then it fades away.

If you get a big enough goal to do something, to achieve something, the Universe will figure out how to do it. But if all you do is set a want and say, "How am I going to go about it?" the Universe is not going to get inspired enough. We need to stimulate the Universe!

Every great success I know has figured out the *why* behind his or her wants, and that's his or her power.

So in our development, we will spend a good amount of energy focusing on why we want these wants, after we've recognized them. Secondly, how are we going to make them happen? We are going to begin from the setting that we can accomplish anything as soon as we have thought it. Anything you yearn for, you must have the belief instantaneously in the feeling of the skill to attain it. That skill is built within us, or we wouldn't have the want in the first place. Come from that point and watch what you can do to create a new certainty of triumph in your life.

Now, I have a question: Do you know why wants really work? Number one, our thoughts are things. Whatever we concentrate on constantly, we experience in our life. If I devote time and thought to one area of my life and I concentrate on it, that is what's going to be real for me. The Universe will manifest.

You can't just write your wants once and never look at them again and really expect things to manifest magically. At least your subconscious mind has a general path to take. But the strength is reviewing them constantly—not obsessively, but on a frequent enough basis that you are directing your subconscious in the right direction. When you set a want, there is an exciting dynamic that occurs. When you set a want, you are acknowledging to your subconscious mind that where you are right now is not where you want to be. You begin to notice the differences between where you want to be and where you are. As you feel that difference, your brain becomes disenchanted. Successful people are always motivated by a sense of unhappiness. When you're completely content, feeling tranquility and gratification, you're not super inspired to do whatever it takes to make things happen. However, when you get frustrated, that's when you get some real strength.

I love disappointment. Disappointment is a strength you want to take full advantage of. It's not something you want to hide yourself from. There is real strength in finding things that you want to move away from because stress is what generates great personalities. Burdens and worry are chief motivators of taking action.

Learning to succeed in managing our burdens and the conflict in our story is one of the essential lessons we all must become skilled at if we want to have a well-adjusted story or if we want to feel really happy and successful.

So what do you want? And why do you want it?

Last time we listed your "I wants." We have some more writing to do!

Now, if you're new to the way of thinking that I teach in this book, which you might be, this is fine. I would like for you to write out everything you want. Literally write out "I want," and then fill in the blanks, no matter how strange they are.

Okay, you have your "I want" list, which I hope is pages and pages long. If you typed it out as a Word document and saved it to "the Cloud," like I did, you can access it anywhere. Technology can be an amazing thing in this day and age.

All right, so you have your wants. Now let's say that your want is: *I want to earn $250,000 per year at my job.*

That's an amazing want. There is nothing wrong with this. Now let's expound on it.

I want to earn $250,000 per year at my job because I want to save enough money for retirement.

Ah, see! There was more to your want. We got the want: a quarter of a million dollars a year. But now, why do you want it? You want to be financially secure for the rest of your life. You want protection. This is great!

I want to attract the man of my dreams because I want someone to love me for me. There is nothing wrong with wanting a man to take care of you, but you want an honest man who will love you in spite of any flaws. It was enough to want something. But now we have to dive deep into your feelings to discover why you actually want it. This will only speed things up to bring them closer to you.

I want to donate a nice portion of my salary to a charity because I want to feel as if I contributed to people in need. Another noble act. You give, and you are going to get a hundredfold in return.

Do you notice the difference with the three examples above? There is a "want" written twice: *I want to open a taco shop because I want my neighborhood to try my great-grandmother's recipe.*

You want something because you want to contribute to someone else. Isn't this what life is all about—setting wants and building upon your wants?

I want *to take my wife and kids to Disneyland because I* want *them to have a memorable vacation.*

Again, *I want...I want.*

You aren't being avaricious. You are creating something for yourself that will affect people you know (and don't know) in a positive light.

I want to get this store to use my product because I want them to feel that my level of service will enhance their shoppers' experience.

You are selling your services to a store, and you are going to make money from the deal. And the entire time you are going to help their shoppers have a great experience because of your services. You will only stand to gain from this type of want, creating a sense of enhancement with other people.

You are creating needs from your wants, and it will only get bigger from here on out. As long as you incorporate a *why* into your *want*, it will keep your goals focused and make you better at fulfilling your dreams.

Also—super important—write out wants for other people you love. A good deed is like a rock plopping in a pond. The ripples will spread far and wide.

So, what do you want—and why? Why is sometimes a more important question than your actual "I want."

I want to live in a beautiful home worth $1.2 million because I want my family to feel comfortable and have enough space to play and eat.

I want to take a vacation with my significant other to Miami because I want her to have a weekend away from work to enjoy herself in a spa.

This is great stuff! But—and this is a *big* but—you can't use these things to the detriment of other people.

I want to own a Patek Phillipe watch worth $25,000 because I want my friends to be jealous of me when I go out with them.

Ugh. Jealousy is a big no-no. If you want something because you want to brag about it, you will only be hurting yourself. No one really cares about what you wear. They will only resent you for it.

I want to coach my son's baseball game because I want him to win a championship so that he can be the best and most popular kid in school.

Okay, there is nothing wrong with wanting to be a champion, but are you doing it for the right reasons? Popularity is never long-term. Do you want to coach your son's team because you want to be a positive role model or because you want to outdo the others? Let's get clear on why you want these things.

I want to make a movie because I want to be rich and famous like the Kardashians.

Ugh. Stop. Please.

You should want to make a movie because you want people to feel the rush of emotions that movies provide, not because you want to walk the red carpet and hobnob with George Clooney. Make a movie because you want to touch people's lives. You should want to affect people for the good. Even if that means that you are creating a horror film. Horror movies make people excited, thrilled, and nervous. Any emotion you can expel on people is a good thing. Just don't do it for the wrong reasons.

So what else do you want? And why do you want it? You can work off your "I want" list or even create a new one. You should be writing constantly. As for me, I write during the first week of every new month. It gives me a list of wants that I can look forward to. If you have what I call "the New Year's syndrome," I suggest that you get over it immediately. As you can probably tell, the New Year's syndrome is when someone wants to make a big change in his or her life starting on January first. It's a new beginning! I must go on this diet. I must pay my bills. I must stop drinking. All these musts become distant verbiage the minute the calendar hits January third. Just three days after the New Year started, what does pretty much everyone do? They revert back to their old ways.

I don't care if it's January third or May third, your "I want" list must be created and reviewed on a consistent basis. You don't need to write every day; it would probably burn you out. Writing can be on a constant rotation. Your wants should be written down at the beginning of the month. And if you have time, which you should, the previous months' "I wants" should be reviewed so that you have a general direction. There can be some wants that changed, and that's fine; just make sure to update them.

Hey, I'm only telling you this because it works, not because I'm some preachy dude. Writing and reviewing your "I wants" monthly keeps them fresh in your head. And because they are fresh in your head, your subconscious can be aware of your goals.

Speaking of your subconscious, you should be giving your commands to it *every night*. Even though your "I wants" are done every few weeks, your subconscious is like a baby. If you don't care for it, it runs wild and begins to talk really stupidly. So we have to keep it in check.

You know that I'm referring to you, of course. Programming your subconscious every night, literally handing off the wants to it, and telling it straight up, "I want to make my new book ranked high on Amazon.com because I want to touch and help people solve their problems all over the world. Okay, so make it happen." I did.

I'll bet that you know what I'm saying to my subconscious tonight, don't you?

No really, command it—right before you go to sleep. If you forget a night or two, no biggie, just jump right back in there. Because it's easy to forget and go backward. It's so easy to start rambling off some negative things that happened to your subconscious mind—and here we go again, back to square one. So really, keep a clear picture of what you want and explain it to your subconscious as if you know that it's going to make it happen. Even if you get off course right when you are falling asleep and you start complaining about your boss or mother-in-law, bring yourself back into focus. Quit the negative chatter and start all over again about your I wants, making sure that your subconscious carries it out.

Also, don't beg or act desperate toward your subconscious. It's a little confusing, and it sounds weird. Be firm—but not annoying. Don't say:

Hi, Andrew (you can name your subconscious anything). I really, really, really, really, really want this girl to call me back because I'm so lonely and she will make me feel, like, so young.

You're subconscious is going cross to its eyes and snarl its upper lip.

Don't confuse your subconscious. Don't come off as desperate either. Remember that your subconscious works for you, not the other way around. Don't say:

Hi, John. I swear, I will really love you if you can just get me this account for my business. I will seriously do anything you want—at any time of the day or night. I really need the money, or my home will be foreclosed, and everyone will think that I'm the laughing stock of the neighborhood.

You're a smart person. You're actually very smart. I'd like to ask you a question. What do you think is going to happen if you speak to your subconscious this way, even though the intention is somewhat good? You need money, but are you asking for it in the correct manner?

Your subconscious is going to hear the desperation in your voice and just make the situation more desperate. It will hear the words *foreclosed* and *laughing stock* and make sure that this is going to happen.

We don't want this to happen! So this is what you should say:

Hi, Jane. I want to thank you for every account you afforded me so far. But here is a big one. I want the account to start using my business because I want to my family and I to be financially free.

Positive talk. Doesn't that sound nicer and more eloquent than the other way?

No: *Hi, Ben. I honestly will be so sad if don't get this raise.*

Yes: *Hi, Brittany. I want to get the raise I deserve because I want to take my friend to the Bahamas as a surprise for her birthday; so make it happen.*

No: *Hi, Chloe. I really, really want a date with this hot guy at work.*

Yes: *Hi, Dawn. I want the nice gentleman at the office to notice me and ask me out on a date. I want him to feel comfortable around me and strike up a conversation at the water cooler.*

No: *Hi, Jason. I want tons of cash stashed in my closet forever.*

Yes: *Hi, Carole. I want an overabundance of wealth to pour into my life and my family's life because I want to be able to buy a really great Mercedes and contribute to people I love.*

No: *Hi, Grace. I want write a movie and sell it to a studio because I want everyone to be envious of my name on a marquee.*

Yes: *Hi, Nancy. I want to open an indie movie theatre with my husband and build a collection of great films to show the neighborhood because I want people to appreciate good cinema.*

So you see, it's all in the delivery of how you do it. It's *why* you want the want that matters most. It's how you ask your subconscious mind. Everything is in your delivery, so deliver it well.

The returns will be magic.

Now, let's go listen to some music!

Chapter 2

The Soundtrack of Your Life

"One good thing about music: when it hits you, you feel no pain."
—Bob Marley

"Do you know what you want? You don't know for sure. You don't feel right, you can't find a cure, and you're getting less than what you're looking for. You don't have money or a fancy car. And you're tired of wishing on a falling star. You gotta put your faith in a loud guitar."
—KISS

"People dancing all in the street. See the rhythm all in their feet. Life is good, wild and sweet. Let the music play on. Feel it in your heart and feel it in your soul. Let the music take control. We're going to party, liming, fiesta, forever. Come on and sing my song!"
—Lionel Richie

Music is wonderful, and I will listen to any type of music. There is a smorgasbord with an endless array of amazing bands and songs spread out across the world: funk, punk, ska, hard rock, hard core, rap, pop, country, opera, classical, world, blues—you name it; I have it.

Music does something to you. It stirs your soul. It gets your creative juices flowing, it makes you feel alive. I know this sounds cliché, but nothing could be further from the truth.

Every Tuesday is new music day on iTunes, and it's a day of the week I cannot wait for. Nothing gets me more pumped than an artist who is about to release his or her next album. I literally count down the days.

But it's not always about new music. I'm constantly pouring over old music I used to listen to. I have three enormous suitcases packed with tapes and CDs—in autobiographical order. If I listen to a certain song, I can tell you the place, who I was with, and what I was doing at that time of that particular song playing. The CDs I've purchased throughout my life are in the order in which I've bought them.

I know it may seem odd, and you're probably saying to yourself now, "Where are you going with this? I mean, what does music have to do with asking the Universe for things?"

It has *everything* to do with it.

Every season—winter, spring, summer, fall—I create a new playlist. I incorporate new music that I'm interested in with some old stuff when I'm in the mood.

Why only make playlists during the season change? Well, for me it's all about that—change. Even though I create my "I want" list monthly, I create my playlist every three months, all titled with the year and season. I have over twenty years of playlists. Some playlists were amazing, and I shared some special times with the artists I was listening to. Some playlists got me through some really tough times. I've had playlists when loved ones passed away. Some playlists were next to me during some great times. I had playlists when I was dating. I've had playlists for the births of my children. I even had a playlist for the day I got married.

The playlist is a very powerful tool because it's a memory that will never die. Isn't that what music does? It creates a memory. It allows you to imprint your subconscious mind with music and match the songs to your surroundings. Your environment, your state, corresponds with the music that you are listening to. You remember things more easily when you can go back to your playlist and listen to the songs on there. You know what type of mood you were in, what you were doing, and how you were feeling. Music will imprint these memories deep in your mind.

When it comes to the types of music you should download, well, I certainly won't preach. My tastes range from one spectrum to the other, so I won't tell you who to listen to. Listen to music that will get you feeling well. Listen to music that will give you goose bumps. It can be any kind—even sad songs.

If you already have a taste in certain music, great! But if you don't, that's okay.

I won't tell you to break the bank and buy every CD or download every song you come across. But if you do, good for you! The more music in your life, the better. But if you are just starting out, no worries. I've got it covered. Pick a band off the top of your head that you have heard of, even in a passing conversation. It can be any artist or any band that you know or that you have heard of—The Beatles, Elvis, Billy Joel, Frank Sinatra, The Ramones, Bo Diddley, Clutch, Mozart, Led Zeppelin, Ozzy Osbourne, 311, Michael Jackson, Jay-Z, Beyonce, Bocelli, Willie Nelson, Madonna,, Pink Floyd, The Rolling Stones, Celine Dion, Garth Brooks, Eminem, Metallica, Taylor Swift, Bon Jovi, Fleetwood Mac, Stevie Wonder, Van Halen, Red Hot Chili Peppers, Green Day, Queen - just to name a few. Go where you can and purchase a couple of albums. Surf the Internet. Ask for recommendations. Then make your playlist. Take a few songs that stick out—you will know them when you hear them because you will want to play them over and over and over again.

The playlist is something that should be created four times a year, in the same manner as your "I want" list. It's something that you have to keep up. Don't just make a playlist on New Year's and be done with it. Make a playlist for the winter season. You can even get into the spirit and throw in some holiday songs, if that's your thing. But when March twentieth arrives, I don't care what type of religion you follow, the weather is going to start getting nicer. It's time for a change. It's time that you create a new playlist. Why? Seasons change. Life changes. You have to keep up. Create something that will make more memories for the spring of that season. Pick new songs. Pick new artists.

Every spring I have a great playlist that coincides with the upping of my age. And no, I'm not frightened of getting older. I'm actually thrilled. It's one of the greatest feelings in the world because I get to learn more. Making a spring playlist is like cleaning out your closet: out with the old winter stuff and in with the new!

After spring, my favorite season arrives—summertime! Who doesn't love the summer? Summer is a time for riding with the windows down, hanging by the beach or pool, and staying out late while it's still light out. The summer playlists are always the best. They seem to carry the most memories.

Then we get into fall. Again, the leaves change; life changes. It's back to school, back to work. Your playlist should reflect that.

If you need some motivation to exercise or simply want to get pumped up about life and you are at a loss of songs to add to your list, you can search the Internet for the best songs to get excited about. There are thousands of these types of songs. I'm assuming that you have a liking, if not a love, for music. If so, make those playlists. They are as important as—if not *more* important than—your "I want" lists.

What—more important than your "I want" list? How is this possible? It's easy. With a diverse and enjoyable playlist to get you moving and thinking for the next few months, nothing can stop you. When you are feeling in a funk or you just can't get your thoughts straight—even with a great "I want" list—pop on those headphones, go to your special place, and start listening to your playlist.

Do you have a plan to create a business? Make a playlist. Have you started dating a person you really like? Create a playlist. Go nuts! Buy as much music as you can afford. Explore different bands. Go deep into iTunes or any type of radio app on your phone and explore the different tastes of music. If you love an artist, find out if there are bands similar to the artist you love. When you find a new band and start to play the music, you will say to yourself, "Where have you been all my life?" Maybe there is a song or two in the band's past that will really speak to your heart. But you have to search for it. It will not just plop into your lap.

When it comes to music as a self-help tool, music is, by far, the greatest pattern interrupter. I cannot tell you how many times I've been down in the dumps over some trivial thing—a breakup with a girlfriend, a loss of an account, a betrayal from a friend—and music was the *only* thing that got my blood flowing again, even when I was writing on my "I want" list. The music that I personally listen to (I have an affection for a four-piece rock and roll band, with loud guitars, a kickin' bass, and banging drums with heavenly vocals) gives me goose bumps. It makes me think. And what do I think? It could be anything, and it could be depending on the song. Some songs make me think about the funny things in life. Some songs make me think about the first time I heard that a girl liked me. Some songs make me think about the first date I went on with my wife. Some songs make me think about the books I want to write. Some songs make me think about where I want to be in the next five years.

When you feel that life isn't giving you a fair shake, put in your ear buds and go listen to your playlist. I am certain that once you get lost in the music, the pattern you were so consumed with moments ago—about how poor your life is headed—is far gone. You should be thinking about other things as your songs progress on your playlist. Let your mind dive into the music and get thinking creatively with it.

Music is power. It will make you feel like a million bucks if you let it. And the real way to get music pumping your blood is to download it and listen to it—on a continual basis.

Since my last book, *The Universe-ity*, I was in a bit of a self-help rut. I wanted to write more, and I did, but nothing was coming out the way it was meant to. I was all over the map, and I didn't have clarity. I started four different manuscripts, but nothing was working. So do you know what I did? I created a great playlist on March twentieth and blasted it on repeat for over two hours while I brainstormed about what I really wanted to say. I want to connect with you. I want my words to let you know that I really care about who you are. I want you to live a fulfilling life, and the reason why I'm writing this, right now, is because I listened to music that motivated me.

If you are ready to make a change in your life, the time is now. You could be a month into the new season, or the new season is just about to start. Regardless, music will get you there. Listen to the music that will make you creative and that will make you feel alive. Create a playlist that you will remember when you listen to it five years later. You will know what you were doing and why you were doing it.

If you want to change your life, create a playlist first, and let the words and the music sink into your subconscious. If you are the creative type and want to write a book or screenplay or write some poetry, think about the characters of the book, the settings, the scenarios. Let the scenes play out in your mind. Let your mind go completely free. There are a billion different roads you can take, and music will take you along any path you want to go if you let it.

Listen to music at night before you go to sleep. Listen to music in your car or on the train on your way into work. Think of yourself in different situations as you listen to your playlist.

I'll never forget some of the best advice I received from a good friend. I always wanted to write a fantasy series, but I had no way to start. The idea was a tiny seedling in my mind, but I would sit at a laptop and just stare at the screen. My friend, who was an author, said that I should create a dynamic playlist. Each song should represent a scene in my book. I followed the advice, created a playlist that coincided with my book, listened to it repeatedly, and thought up different scenarios and different angles to play. A few weeks later, I had a two-hundred-page manuscript. Listen to songs that will keep you alert and that will allow your subconscious mind to work wonders through your fingers. Have songs that will inspire you to do something creative.

A few years later, a different friend of mine was trying to write a novel. I gave her the same advice that I received, and, guess what? She's now a best-selling author!

Now I'm not saying that by creating a playlist you will become a novelist. But what I am saying is that making a great list of songs you like for the certain season in your life will only have its rewards. This can apply to any area of your life. If you want to succeed at work and need a little jolt, listen to music. If you want to connect with your kids, introduce them to music you listen to and listen together. If you want to be more creative—whether its writing a book or building a website—listen to music!

Especially if you have thought long and hard all day about a problem, putting on some music can become an incubation period for your ideas. The subconscious mind has been working extremely hard to solve the problems that you face, and now that you let your mind wander while listening to music, it can surface and plant those ideas into your conscious mind.

You don't even realize this, but you are actually visualizing when you listen to music. You are visualizing what you want your life to be like. It's another way of connecting your subconscious mind with the Universe. Granted, you are listening to the music as it plays, but most importantly, you are thinking out of your element. You can be in a bad mood, but put on a great song, and, boom, it snaps you out of your funk. What would you rather be impregnating your subconscious mind with: thoughts of misery and anger or thoughts of thrills and excitement? You know the answer. Music will get you there.

If you get sick of a song, simply fast forward it or skip the track. As for me, I have about thirty to forty songs per playlist—sometimes even more. These should be enough to get your blood flowing over the next few months.

Oh, and for the people out there in the Universe who say that they don't have time for this, you don't have my pity. I'm at my office at 6:00 a.m. every day, and then my second shift begins when I get home to play with my kids. After the kids go to sleep, its music time, baby!

Of course, you have time to listen to music! Everyone has time to listen to music. You have to make time. You can take a walk or just sit on your couch and let the music seep in. Trust me when I tell you that it will change your state and make you feel alert—much like how the "I want" list does. There is no telling where the music will take you. It's as if you have a wide-open roadmap, and the songs will guide you along your path.

I love hearing from you, and I certainly want to hear about the music you listen to, so please e-mail me your wonderful playlists. I want to know what types of music excite you and get your juices flowing.

Michael@samuelsbooks.com

Chapter 3

Keep Calm and Ask On

"Every time I think I got it figured, something bigger always jumps in the frame, something gets in the way. Now I'm ready to turn the page on yesterdays and forgive them. Now I'm willing to disengage, to seize the day and move on."

—311

"Fear is the path to the dark side. Fear leads to anger. Anger leads to hate. Hate leads to suffering."

—Yoda

So we know why we want the things we do. We know that everyone wants things. We know that adding more to your "I want" list is key for you to reach your goals. And we also learned that music has a lot of power over us and helps us to visualize our future.

"All the world's a stage, and all the men and women merely players. They have their exits and their entrances, and one man in his time plays many parts...."

Shakespeare certainly had it right, didn't he? Don't worry, this isn't a book about Shakespeare. This is a book about life— about being your true self and fulfilling your dreams.

We all are different people at different times in our lives: a person is a son or daughter, a brother or sister, a father or mother, a grandfather or grandmother, an uncle or an aunt, a friend, a boss, an employee, a hero, a creator.

All of these aspects create us, and we often play these "roles" at the same time. We enter others' lives to accomplish something good or bad, and then we depart. Our lives also change as we grow and gain wisdom. What we did in our first act is not the same as in our third; even though the situation may be the same, we have changed. Our role is different. We have more knowledge, more experience. We have other people in our lives.

"All the world's a stage" is the phrase that begins a prologue from *As You Like It*, spoken by the melancholy Jaques in Act II Scene VII.

Jaques's famous speech compares life with theatre. Are we just living life to a script preordained by a higher order—perhaps the Universe?

Now for the knotty part.

Every story has a villain. Meaning, in your life, in your story, you are going to come across people who are just straight-up mean and evil and will want to see you flounder.

No, wait, this isn't a negative book. You know I only speak the truth to you. But now for the good news—and remember this:

The bigger the bad guy, the bigger the obstacles that are thrown in your path, the bigger the reward for you.

Do me a favor and highlight that on your Kindle, please.

Write that on a Post-it note and put it on your work computer.

Live by these words because it's a universal truth:

The bigger the enemy, the bigger the obstacle, the bigger the reward.

You can highlight that, too, because it's that important.

The more people who are against you, the more people who want to see you fail, and the more people who want to bring you down, it will only get you closer to the thing you so desire. Never forget this.

Things are going to happen. I know—discouraging, right? I want you to know that life isn't always puppy dogs and unicorns. Sometimes someone is going to try to spoil your production. Someone is going to plan to ruin everything you are trying to do.

Why? I have no idea. People who want to see other people fail are just not awakened to the ideas of the Universe. If I could eradicate negative people or setbacks in my life, I would choose to. But where would that get me? Nowhere.

Have you ever seen the film *Rounders*, with Matt Damon? If not, I highly recommend it. It's in my top five favorite movies of all time. What would life be like if Matt Damon's character plodded along in law school and played poker for a living—never getting into trouble, never getting into adventures with Worm, just...playing...poker and winning (every hand), with nothing else happening?

It's boring! The Universe knows that this is boring. That's why the Universe puts setbacks and annoying people in your path. It wants to see if you are going to react the right way to get to your desired goal. That's why we have to keep calm and ask on in any type of adversity.

Hindrances and frustrating people are aggravating, but they are part of life. The best part about them is that they make you grow. Their negativity actually makes you awaken further. It gives you obstacles to overcome. Annoying people make you think. They make you plot ways to get around their obstacles.

The bigger someone or something is going to make an obstacle for you to overcome, the bigger your prize or "I want" is going to be.

Nothing in life comes easy because if it did, it would be boring. Victory is only sweet when we sweat.

What is worse than a novel about a guy who wakes up and has everything he wants? And for the next four hundred pages, we just read about this guy getting everything that he wants: he wins the lotto; he marries the perfect girl; he has great kids; he never gets sick, never catches a cold. So what would happen if we read a story where the person gets everything he or she wants? We'd all be asleep! Who wants to read something like this?

Don't we want to see a guy who has everything trading place with a guy who has nothing to see how their behavior would be? Remember the film *Trading Places* with Dan Akroyd and Eddie Murphy? It wasn't about watching a man lose everything; it was about who this person became when he realized that you don't know what you've got till it's gone. These are the types of stories that make our lives so much more interesting. Each one of us has these stories.

There are highs and lows in stories, just like in real life, because that is what life is. The highs are great and last a long time. But there are lows. Everyone has lows. It doesn't matter who you are; you have experienced a low point in your life. Whether it was a breakup with a girlfriend, a stomach virus (blech), or losing a loved one. We all experience pain.

The key here is this: are you going to finish your story and come out on top, or are you going to succumb to the "dark side?" Are you going to drown in your self-pity, or are you going to be triumphant and seize the day?

Are you going to keep calm and ask on?

Are you going to give up on your desires or your wants because one thing didn't go your way?

Are you going to let the bad guy spoil your win? Name any story that the bad guy won. Although you think that by the "dark night of the soul" moment in any story that the bad guy has his arsenal together, there is no way in hell that the good guy is going to overcome this. They are surrounded by flesh-eating zombies! A great white shark just sank their boat! Gollum just bit off Frodo's finger—*with the ring*! The Joker just took Gotham hostage. Buzz and Woody are stuck at that vicious kid Sid's house and are about to be mauled by his dog. Harry Potter, er...I actually have no idea what happens to Harry Potter in any of the films because I've never seen a Harry Potter film. But I will bet you anything that near the end of the story, you think something horrible is going to happen to Harry, but he reaches deep, *deep* down and pulls out that last bit of energy to fight off the bad guy, save the people of his land, and get the girl. Am

I right, or am I right? I've never even seen it, but I know he wins. He has to win. We all have to win! Why? Because we're the good guys! And the good guys always win.

I hope you're not an antagonist. I really hope for your own sake that you aren't intentionally hurting people and making them feel any less significant than they really are. Bad guys are called that—bad guys— for a reason. And guess what? They always lose in the end. Even if they feel that they are going to win and beat the protagonist (you), they will never come out on top because that is not how the Universe works.

Bad guys don't win in any story. Good guys win. Even if it may not look that way. The good guy must go through hell and back to get the outcome he desires. The good guy must metaphorically perish before being reborn again. It happens in *every* story.

You may feel that your life stinks. But there is something you can do to reevaluate the position you are in. Who are the bad guys in your life? Who is holding you down? Who is rooting for your downfall? Who are the people in your life that don't want you to succeed? Who in your life is forcing his or her will upon you?

It could be a boss, a coworker, a friend, or even a family member. It's unfortunate, but these people exist, and they're everywhere. The Universe has put them in your script of life to teach you who you really are. So, who are you? Get out your journal because we are going to do some writing here.

A protagonist always has positive people that surround him or her: a good friend, a brother, sister, mother, father, son, daughter, cousin, uncle, or aunt. I am very fortunate to have all of these. I surround myself with my family members, who are constantly rooting for me and supporting my goals.

Who in your life is supporting you? Don't say you that don't have anyone. It doesn't exist, unless you live by yourself on Jupiter.

People like you. They are out there. Someone is supporting you; someone likes you; someone loves you. Someone is rooting for your best interest. Who is that person? Seek him or her out and align yourself with that person on your quest. Work to become a better friend, lover, partner, brother, sister, uncle, aunt—whatever. Whatever role you play in the person's life that is supporting your endeavors, make him or her your friend and partner. Tell your subconscious about this great person because he or she won't abandon you. That individual will make you feel worthy.

Now, what about the people who are rude, abusive, and don't support anything you do? Should you hang around them? Listen to their ideas? Play their games?

It's sad to see someone, especially someone you love, who is constantly negative. There isn't anything you can do for that person. You can try, gingerly, to introduce him or her to a great spiritual book that will maybe open his or her eyes to their negativity. But don't bet on it. I know, I wish I had better news. You can't change people. Negative people are who they are. Don't try to change it. You can, however, be thankful that they are in your life because they are teaching you a valuable lesson.

They are teaching you to be a better you. If you are reacting negatively to their bad behavior, you are just going to their level. You have to rise above them. Don't stoop to the negative person's level. They will beat you with experience. Put on your bulletproof negativity vest and become impervious to their idiotic quips.

Quick story: One day Buddha was walking through a village. A very angry and rude young man came up and began insulting him, saying all kinds of rude words.

The Buddha was not upset by this verbal abuse. Instead, he asked the young man, "Tell me, if you buy a gift for someone and that person does not take it, to whom does the gift belong?"

The young man was surprised to be asked such a strange question and answered, "It would belong to me because I bought the gift."

The Buddha smiled and said, "That is correct. And it is exactly the same with your anger. If you become angry with me and I do not get insulted, then the anger falls back on you. You are then the only one who becomes unhappy, not me. All you have done is hurt yourself."

I wanted to discuss this story briefly because I've recently had the chance to experience something that proved to me that this is a very true and practical tool to apply every day in all different types of scenarios.

A client of mine was plain rude and said some very derogatory comments about me. I could have easily told him to go suck on an egg, but I wouldn't have been any better than he was. I sympathized with this client's pain and understood where he was coming from. I offered to make up the poor service, and if he wouldn't take what I was offering, it was his problem now. He calmed down and dropped the subject.

The thing I want to stress here is that, just like in the story of the Buddha, I didn't accept his "gift." I actually felt sorry for him. I didn't feel like his words had anything to do with me, although he was looking at me, and he addressed them to me.

And looking back he actually gave me something precious: he gave me the opportunity to experience, for a tiny bit, what that Buddha story said. And I felt great noticing that I didn't allow that to change my feeling, to change the exuberant state I was in. I continued going about my day, asking the Universe "How does it get any better than this?"

Every day we have so many people around us, bringing us gifts that are sometimes concealed in ugly packages. Some packages are really nice and pretty. You always have the choice. You can accept or not accept these gifts. It's as simple as that. If you accept the negative gift and react to this person's negativity, you are no better than he or she is. However, there are people looking to give you gifts that will only enhance your life. If you take these gifts, you will rise above the muck and become a better person. There are going to be supporting cast members throughout your life who are going to really like you. Stay with them. Bounce ideas off of them.

Write their names in your journal and thank the Universe for them. Write something like:

I am grateful for my wife, Sharon, in my life.

I am grateful for my mom, Phyllis, in my life.

I am grateful for my brother, Eric, in my life.

Write about the people in your orbit—the people you surround yourself with. Make sure that they are people that root for you: people that you can call when the chips are down; people that will give you an honest answer if you ask them (that is key). People in your orbit who truly love you can tell you that you are doing something wrong. It doesn't make them annoying or wrong. And you shouldn't react to it. You should be grateful for the constructive criticism. People who love you should be able to criticize you, and you shouldn't get offended. You should be thankful that someone cares about you enough to tell you something that you didn't know you were doing. Trust me when I say that I've had my fair share of constructive criticism. You have to be able to identify when someone is telling you that you are doing something wrong that could hurt you.

Negative people and their unpleasant attitudes are very, very different from constructive criticism. Constructive criticism is not an attack on you. It's simply telling you something that you should use to improve yourself. Negative people talk badly behind your back. They are happy when you fail. They laugh when you are not well. They are happy when you get sued. They are not supportive of you when you need them to be. That is different from not agreeing when you are doing something that doesn't seem right. Just because someone doesn't agree with you doesn't make him or her a bad person. It just means he or she has a difference of opinion, which is perfectly fine and normal. Negative people try to stop you from growing.

If you live with a negative person and you are unhappy, I am by no means telling you to leave or divorce that person. When we commit to someone in marriage, I firmly believe that we commit for life. I don't believe in severing relationships. I believe in solutions. What are solutions when living with someone who is a misery? Get busy. Do something constructive. Surround them (and yourself) with a white light and go about your day. Pray for that person that his or her soul finds peace in this world, and then go pick up a book on spirituality. Or better yet, write your life's work and self-publish it. Don't feed the negativity by feeling sorry for yourself. Get your life and your affairs in order and do something that will feed your soul: you can exercise, read a book, write a book, watch a movie, or listen to a playlist. (we covered that in Chapter 2, remember?)

If you are stuck in this type of negative relationship, find solace in something else. Don't let that negative person bring you down. Better yourself, and that negative person may actually take notice. There is a small chance that he or she will want to change, but there is still that tiny chance he or she will begin to get interested in what you are doing.

Set an example for someone who is negative. And don't ever be the victim. Having a "poor me" attitude will only impress that type of feeling on your subconscious mind, and your subconscious will ensure that it brings more "poor me" situations to your life.

But really, how does a good guy in a story overcome the bad guy? Not by avoiding that person but by impressing his ideas onto that individual. Okay, sometimes it doesn't work. Some people aren't going to change. But that shouldn't stop you from reaching your goals and fulfilling your dreams. They will try to stop you. Push their negative energy away from you and move on. They can't stop you. Nothing will! The only person that can stop you is *you*! You are the only thing that is hindering you from getting what you want. The negative person is just there. He or she is hot air. Hot air can't hurt you unless you let it. I actually like hot air. It feels good when it hits your skin. But if you don't like hot air, change your pattern when the hot air is blown your way. Your confidence becomes invincible. You can even try to change the negative person's pattern.

How do you change your pattern?

At night, right before you fall asleep, ask your subconscious mind for help. Tell your subconscious that you want to see dancing leprechauns farting gold on rainbows when the antagonist is trying to defeat your dreams. When someone is condemning you, those leprechauns are going to come dancing right into your view and farting up a storm. They are going make you laugh inwardly, and you will not hear any of the negative words being spewed in your direction.

Think of something as funny (I don't know what could be more funny than dancing leprechauns farting gold on a rainbow over the head of someone who is screaming at the top of his or her lungs!) that will make you smile deep down in your gut.

However, my favorite pattern interrupter is dressing up the "screamer" in my mind. Remember these crucial steps when being lambasted by a shrieking baboon:

Dress him or her up as a clown! Mentally dress that person in a long polka dot jacket, with or without tails. The pants could be short, long, or oversized. I prefer oversized. You can choose from a wide selection of colorful plaids, stripes, polka dots, and checks as well as solid colors. Commonly called "the tailor's nightmare," the costume colors and patterns should complement the overall clown appearance, whether or not they are color-coordinated or not matching. Not matching seems funnier. The costume can be complemented with outlandish accessories, like: large or small ties, vests, colorful socks, large or comical collars, suspenders, and many styles and colors of comical clown shoes. These and one of the many hat possibilities—like skimmers, Irish derbies, bowlers, top hats, stovepipes, "mad hatters," and "crushables"—in various bright colors will enhance the clown character. White or colored gloves are also worn.

Then I picture that person's face painted in clown makeup. He or she has a highly colorful makeup with a pink-based flesh tone on the face and neck. The eye and nose area are usually covered in white to produce a wide-eyed expression and to emphasize the mouth design. Designs in and around the eyes and mouth are generally black or red, but other lining colors, in moderation, are acceptable. A red shadowing around the nose area is generally outlined in black. This clown will normally wear a large comical nose appropriate to the size of the clown's face. He or she is wearing a big dopey wig, but you can choose from the many varied styles and colors to accentuate the costume and flesh tone of your screamer. Dress him or her up!

Even if you crack a smile when you are in a negative person's company, it's okay. The bad person is probably gonna say, "What's so funny?"

Then tell him or her something funny that happened to you. But it must be really funny: like the time a fly flew into your ear at a busy shopping center parking lot! Or bring up something funny that someone or something else did. Remember when your dog fell asleep on the couch, rolled over and fell off of it, and then trotted away like nothing happened? Or, get this one: your friend was finished with her cup of coffee, and instead of rolling down the front window of her car, she rolled down the back seat window and threw the coffee out the front, splashing all over the front seat?

I'll never forget when my daughter, on her first birthday, was eating pasta in our favorite Italian family style restaurant. She got really full and flung the pasta onto another old couple's table while they were eating soup!

That's funny.

By the time you are done telling your extremely funny story to this negative person, chances are that he or she is probably going to forget what he or she was screaming at you about. Release your laughter and let it out.

Turn the negativity in your life into something funny. Beat the bad guy with laughter and kindness. Let him know that you are not affected one iota from their bad places. Just don't tell him about the farting leprechauns.

Now, on to a really funny chapter.

Chapter 4

LOL: Law of Laughing

"There is little success where there is little laughter."
—Andrew Carnegie

"Life literally abounds in comedy if you just look around you."
—Mel Brooks

"I am thankful for laughter, except when milk comes out of my nose."
—Woody Allen

All right, all right, I know what you're thinking. Mike, c'mon man, this is the law of attraction. You shouldn't be talking about anything funny. You certainly can't make fun of it. The law of attraction is not funny! It's very serious! All of those book covers are very, very, *very* serious. They're full of mystical words and verbiage, ancient symbols, and night skies with shooting stars. There are angels on the covers and the faces of very serious authors. There is nothing funny about that.

Why is everyone so serious when reading a book on the law of attraction?

I need a big favor—really big. I'm going to require you to do something throughout the remainder of this book.

Well, yeah, I am gonna force something on you.

I'm going to force you to smile.

Gasp! What? Smile? Me? How could I smile? I'm reading this book to get advice on using the law of attraction. I said that there is nothing funny about the law of attraction. It's very serious!

When was the last time you read a law of attraction book and actually smiled? I've smiled through lots of them, but they were more of those "aha" smiles. There weren't really any funny smiles.

Smiling and laughing during a law of attraction book is like cracking up on jury duty while the defense is putting on its case. It's serious. You can't laugh. It's not meant to be funny. Law of attraction books are meant to be taken seriously. They are meant to be real, raw, edgy, spiritual. But none of them are funny. And if there is a funny LOA book, please send it my way.

I'm not going to dissect why law of attraction books aren't funny. The authors of these books are teaching you one thing without doing the most important thing, allowing you, the reader, to have the time of your life by reading their book.

I believe that anyone who is so serious when talking about the law of attraction isn't doing it the right way. So the next time you read a book with absolutely no sense of humor, take heed. *Keep Calm and Ask On* is a first of its kind.

There is more to life than taking everything so seriously. You create the life you want. But if you're going to be serious about it, you'll be headed nowhere fast.

You may be saying to yourself right now, "I'm just so stressed. I have bills to pay! I have children screaming! I have a deadline on a term paper! When, in the name of the Universe, can I possibly find time to smile and laugh?"

My answer: *right now!*

Let's relax those shoulders. Stretch that neck out. Loosen up the cheeks. Let your teeth shine through. Let's have some fun. Let's laugh. Laugh out loud at the silliness that life really is. Maybe life is all too easy, and we are putting too much thought into it. Jimmy Buffet once said:

Maybe it's all too simple
For our brains to figure out.
What if the hokey pokey
Is all it really is about?

Makes you think, doesn't it? Is this some cosmic joke that we can all laugh about? If the Universe gave us our greatest asset we have, laughter, are we using it enough? Or are we instead using the other stuff—negative thoughts, depressing moods, stress—to go about our day?

I've discovered a new law. It's called the law of laughter. And it's in the same vein as the law of attraction.

Laws are meant to be taken seriously, but you can still have fun with them. You shouldn't break laws. That's not funny. But playing with laws and using them for your benefit will shape you into a different person—a person that you want to become.

True, there are tons of people that became amazingly successful by being a curmudgeon, a killjoy, a wet blanket. But who wants to copy their life? I certainly don't. And I hope you don't either.

So, what's so funny about the law of attraction? Well, for starters, you have to relax and know that the Universe is conspiring on your behalf. That should take the edge off. But you knew that already.

You should also be super happy that you have a best friend with you 24-7-365: your subconscious. You can go to your friend any time of the day (I prefer evenings right before bedtime). And you can ask your friend for anything to carry out, and he or she usually does. Nice!

Now, this is super important. Look up— straight up. A grin from ear to ear. If you don't have ears, I want that smile to stretch all the way around until the corners of your lips touch.

Are you there? Good? Now, as you are smiling straight up into the sky, I want you to start laughing—not a forced throat laughter. I'm talking about from your gut.

As you're laughing and smiling, I want you to run down the things you are grateful for. What in your life, as you laugh and smile, could you be grateful for? What is making you laugh and smile at this instant? Is it your kids? I know that my children bring a smile to my face every single time I think of them. What about your boyfriend, girlfriend, spouse, or significant other? Does he or she make you smile? I know that when I'm down in the dumps, I can think of some wild adventures I've had with my wife, and it brings a big smile to my face. What about with friends? Can you think of a time that you had a ball with your friends? Laughter is subjective. What is funny to one person is not funny to another. Find your funny spot and laugh!

It's these little moments that we need to stop and think about, to reflect on. We need to pause, smile, and laugh at the joy life really brings.

What could make you laugh? How about a good movie. My all-time favorite comedy is *Back to School*. Rodney Dangerfield was brilliant. What movie would make you smile? What type of music would make you smile? We covered playlists and music already, but I can certainly name songs that make me laugh and smile. Those memories I had growing up listening to those songs bring me back. They ground me. What about you? Are there any songs that can make you physically smile? Any concerts you've been to that can make you smile?

You must do this! Look up into the sky, smile, and laugh. You aren't laughing at the Universe; you're giving it what it wants: a great feeling, a good attitude. The Universe wants to hear your laughter constantly. It's a feeling of being grateful. People can say that they are grateful, but they have to smile and laugh to be grateful.

It's easy to say, "I'm grateful" and go about your day. But is your whole body feeling it? You have to feel your laugh. From your toes to your fingernails, every pore of your body should feel your laugh. Laugh till you cry. Laugh till your sides hurt. Really give it a go. Think of the most outrageous thing you have done and laugh about it. Please note: do not think about something you did illegally and didn't get caught. That's not funny. My old man has always said, "You can do something illegal one hundred times, but you only can get caught once." So don't think about bad things you've done. Think about the good things you've done—funny things you've done.

This may be too simple—again, I like simplicity—but I want you to look up and smile and laugh twice a day for thirty days. While laughing, take deep breaths in and let out the laugh when you exhale. As you take deeps breaths, you are inhaling good feelings and comedy. As you exhale, you are releasing all of the negative feelings trapped in your body.

Do each exercise for about a minute or two. It shouldn't last too long. But think of all the things that you have gratitude for—anything that will bring a smile to your face. I'm not talking about a smirk; I'm talking about a full-on smile.

You will not regret this.

The Greeks said that laughter is of the gods. Laughter is a medicine for many predicaments. Do you realize that men and women are the only beings in this world that can laugh? Animals can't laugh. Fish can't laugh. There has to be a reason for this. The

Universe gave you the option to laugh—do it!

Laughter restores your viewpoint and lets you think vibrantly and definitively. Make it a purpose to laugh at your fears. Be sure to laugh when people aggravate you, and by all means, laugh at all the thoughtless, trivial mistakes you made today.

Laugh at yourself for being so serious and stuffy. The bigger the problem, the more comedy you need. Self-pity and blame are eradicated when your laughter takes over.

I once made my son a delicious omelet with ham and cheese. I poured some milk for him and set it on the kitchen table. He sat down and accidentally knocked over the milk and omelet onto the kitchen floor. Instead of bawling his eyes out, he laughed. There really is no use in crying over spilled milk.

Chapter 5

Team Universe

"Find joy in everything you choose to do. Every job, relationship, home…. It's your responsibility to love it or change it."
—Chuck Palahniuk

"Love yourself first and everything else falls into line. You really have to love yourself to get anything done in this world."
—Lucille Ball

"There are two ways to live: you can live as if nothing is a miracle; you can live as if everything is a miracle."
—Albert Einstein

This final chapter is a bookend to the beginning. In the first chapter, I discussed wants and the fact that everyone has them. It doesn't matter who you are; your life is filled with wants every second of the day. But what you may not understand is that in order to be content with what you have, you technically have all you need. I know that is somewhat contradictive, but it really balances out my theory. There is nothing wrong with wanting more, but you will get more when the Universe decides that you are ready to receive it.

People feel that they lack. They think that they asked the Universe for something, and they didn't get it. The Universe has actually given you exactly what you need for the time that you are in—right now.

You may need more of something next month or next year, and when that time comes around, the Universe will make sure that it happens. You don't have to worry. The Universe will make sure that you have it when you need it. Trust the Universe. If you don't have it right now, don't fight it and don't be upset; you don't need it right now. Your wants will come into your life when you need them.

You should feel content. You should feel that you are not "less than." You have what you need for today. The Universe wasn't having a bad day today because it didn't give you what you wanted when you wanted it. The Universe doesn't have bad days. Whew, that's a relief!

Take what you have and do the most with it. If we had a bigger building, I'd be happier. If we had a bigger home, I'd be happier. You have the talent and experience to manifest everything you want. It may not be as much as someone else, but you shouldn't be competing with him or her anyway. You should be competing with yourself. Are you becoming the best person you can possibly be?

People do not determine your destiny. People cannot stop the Universe's plan for what's in store for your life. You command your subconscious mind and answer to the Universe—not people.

You have what you need for today. Take what you have and make the most of it. You've survived; you're here. Stop thinking about what things would be like if they were different. This is all that you need now. Don't sit around with a defeatist attitude. When it's time to get what you want, nothing can stand in between you and your destiny. Don't feel shortchanged. The Universe has already lined up the right people, the right prospects, and the right protection for you.

Thank the Universe, and it will give you what you need, when you need it. Even though a dream hasn't come to fruition, will you keep a good attitude? If you have trust in yourself and the Universe, you will get everything you need.

If you had needed more money, more support, more vacations, the Universe would have given it to you. The moment it becomes "not enough," the Universe will give you more. The Universe will show up when someone interferes with your destiny. Don't be downcast that it won't work out. When you need it, it won't be one second late. It *will* show up. You are part of this amazing Universe. It's watching out for you. The Universe is directing your steps and giving you what you need, as long as you continue to respect it.

Stop being stressed out. The Universe has planned every day of your life. If you don't have something now, as long as you are devoting a sense of gratitude to the Universe and respecting it, when you need the thing you want, the Universe will always deliver. If it hasn't happened yet, don't sit around with an unpleasant attitude. Have confidence. Remember: you don't want to be the bad guy. The bad guy always loses.

You are just looking at the ordinary existence. But the Universe is bigger than that. The Universe is magical. It surrounds us and binds us all together. It's in everything that you cannot see.

The Universe will make a way for you, even if you don't see it. You are not at a minus. Use what you have, and the Universe will multiply it. It will explode. I can attest to this. Everything I have in my life has grown a hundredfold since I put all my faith in the Universe. The Universe will never ask you to do something and then not give it to you if you couldn't do it. The moment the Universe put the dream in your heart, it lined up everything in the correct order to give to you.

Also, don't make excuses. Don't sit on the sidelines of life. Put your wants into the Universe's hands and have trust that it's working. Don't maintain a negative attitude. Be thankful. Be joyous. Have gratitude about everything that you have received, everything in your life, and everything that you are going to get.

Now, regarding competition, here are my thoughts: *there is no such thing as competition.* You are your own person. The Universe gives you what you need. If the Universe gave you what your competitors had, it would hinder you, not help you. What the Universe gave other people will not work for you. Don't be like someone else. You are unique—one of a kind. You are custom-made. Be yourself. You can have less talent and resources, but if you believe in the Universe, you will go further than people with more talent and more resources.

Don't dismiss what the Universe has given you. When you realize that what you have has been made for you—it wasn't a random happening—you should be all the more grateful. The Universe matched you for your world.

The same goes true for your subconscious. Learn to believe in the workings of your subconscious mind, knowing that whatever you impress on your subconscious will be expressed in your reality. Whatever you mentally accept and feel to be true will come to pass. The way that you really think and feel deep down in your heart rules all phases of your life. If you are happy, you will lead a happy life. If you think riches, you will be rich—not just monetarily but by all different kinds of riches.

I believe that *luck* is a very good word if you put a "p" before it. The person who believes that luck controls his or her destiny will be waiting for quite some time for his or her want to show up. The individual will lie in bed, hoping that they will get an e-mail that they have won the lottery. The creator shapes his or her future by their attitude. Those individuals know that they are born to prosper, and that they are equipped to be winners. They are diligent, passionate, and conscientious about the job they're doing, and they whistle while they work. The person who thinks about luck usually whines and grumbles about his or her life. Luck relies on chance. Successful people rely on attraction, and attraction is destiny.

No matter how bad the situation, you can turn it around and profit by it. You can make an opportunity out of every problem to service life and rise higher.

All of your fear and anxieties are caused by your belief in external powers. All of this is based on being unaware of the truth about the Universe.

Many people scoff at the notion that there is a Universe, that the supply of wants and good things is limited. These people insist that government must be changed before anyone can acquire what he or she desires.

This is simply not true.

If you truly are on "Team Universe" and have the advancing mind, have trust that they can get everything their heart desires and move forward with the fixed purpose to become what they want to be. Nothing, absolutely nothing, can keep them down.

Anyone can follow the rules in this book and create the life he or she wants under any government, and still get all of his or her wants.

The more people who compete against each other for their wants will only delay their journey. It is enough to know that neither the government under which you live nor the capitalistic markets can keep you from your wants. When you become a creator, the Universe will allow you to rise above the so-called competition level that people clamor in and live a life that only you can dream about.

Remember: your thoughts must be held in a level with what your subconscious will carry out. And you are never for an instant to be swayed that the supply is limited. The Universe will make whatever you need as long as you think in the particular way I've outlined here.

Whenever you do fall into the old ways of thought, don't panic. Keep calm. Correct yourself immediately. When you feel that you are starting to compete with others, center your mind, pick up this book, and revert back to your "I want" list. Even go so far as to mentally think about it during the day. Add more wants to your list. Just don't compete with others.

Also, don't spend any time planning how you will meet a conceivable crisis in the future—except, of course if something may be affecting your actions today. If you are navigating a boat and see an iceberg, steer clear of it. But if you are about to board a ship, don't worry about the iceberg. If you are driving and see a gaggle of geese, try to maneuver your vehicle so that you don't hit them. But if you are getting into your car, don't wonder if you are going to hit a goose today.

Does this make sense?

You should be thinking about doing today's work in an effective manner and not about emergencies that may arise tomorrow. You can deal with them if they come.

But don't question yourself about how you are going to surmount these castle-in-the-sky obstacles that may loom upon your personal, professional, or social horizon unless you can see plainly that your course must be altered today in order to avoid them.

No matter how big a barrier may appear at a distance, you will find that if you have trust in the Universe and command your subconscious mind in the correct manner, the looming problem will disappear as you approach it. Or, a way over, through, or around it will appear. Take this way instead.

No possible arrangement of circumstances can defeat you. Every difficulty carries with it the ability to overcome it. So relax.

Watch your tongue. Never speak of yourself, your relationships, your dealings, or of anything else in a disappointing way. Never admit the likelihood of failure or speak in a way that implies failure as a possibility.

Times may be hard, or business conditions may be doubtful for those who compete, but they can never be so for you. You can create what you want. You are above fear.

When others are having a hard time and poor business, you will find your greatest opportunities.

Train yourself to think of and to look upon this great world as growing and to regard seemingly evil people as being only those who are undeveloped.

Always speak in terms of advancement. Never allow yourself to feel disappointed. You may expect to have a certain thing at a certain time and not get it at that time; this will feel like a failure to you. But if you hold to your trust, you will find that failure is only a stepping-stone to getting what you really want. Keep calm, and if you do not receive that thing, something so much better will fall in your lap that seeming failure was really a success in disguise.

Do not read pessimistic or conflicting literature or get into arguments upon the matter.

The thinker does not give power to things, conditions, people, or circumstances. He or she is full of grace, balance, and calmness because that individual knows that his or her thoughts and feelings impress and shape his or her destiny. Do not be afraid of anything or any person, for the only enemies that you can ever have are your negative or fearful thoughts.

William James said, "Believe in the good life and believe that life is worth living, and your belief will cause this to become a fact."

And most importantly, always remember to keep calm and ask on.

Outro

"We humans have lost the wisdom of genuinely resting and relaxing. We worry too much. We don't allow our bodies to heal, and we don't allow our minds and hearts to heal."
—Thich Nhat Hanh

"A man of calm is like a shady tree. People who need shelter come to it."
—Toba Beta

"The pursuit, even of the best things, ought to be calm and tranquil."
—Marcus Tullius Cicero

Whew! We made it! We finished the book together. I cannot begin to tell you how grateful I am to have the opportunity to serve you. We are pals, and I will never forget this experience.

I hope that you take the ideas in *Keep Calm and Ask On* in a way that will only make your life better. I want you to enjoy the life that you were given.

Please know that this isn't the end. I'm not going anywhere. When life throws you a curve ball, my books are here to help lift your spirits. Remember the principles laid out here. They are universal and timeless. I only say this because I want the best from you. I truly do. You deserve to acquire whatever you need, whenever you need it. You should have the power, capability, and trust in yourself that you can accomplish anything. The world and everything in it is yours. I know that sounds cliché, but it couldn't be further from the truth. Make your name here. Build your future by asking the Universe and commanding your subconscious mind. Live the life you were meant to live.

Keep your head in check and never stoop to the level of people who want to bring your hopes down. Rise above the issues and press forward to sculpt the life you are intended to live. Don't worry about what other people may think. If they don't understand these principles, that's fine. All that matters is if you understand the principles of the Universe.

The Universe wants to give you everything you need. Fulfill your dreams and feel the power come through you.

Command your subconscious. Don't let it command you. If a nasty thought is brought out, cast it aside and press forward with your approach.

I know that I'm not reinventing the wheel here. The law of attraction is still the law of attraction. But I want you to have fun with it. Write down those "I wants" frequently. Listen to music. Keep calm. Laugh a lot. And remember, you are on Team Universe here! There is no better team to align yourself with.

About the Author

With a degree in English, a second degree in Finance, a Master's in business administration, and a PhD from The Universe-ity, Michael Samuels has attracted everything into his life because he followed successful people and their thought ideologies. He has read and thoroughly applied hundreds of books on spirituality, self-improvement, and the law of attraction to his life. The Universe has helped Michael run a highly successful family business with offices all over the country. He currently lives in New York with his wife, son, and daughter.

Michael would love to hear from you! Please e-mail him your stories about how the Universe fulfilled your dreams.

E-mail: michael@samuelsbooks.com

Website: www.samuelsbooks.com

14444511R00073

Printed in Great Britain
by Amazon.co.uk, Ltd.,
Marston Gate.